I've Lost My Hat

Written by Charnan Simon
Illustrated by Rick Stromoski

Children's Press®
A Division of Scholastic Inc.
New York • Toronto • London • Auckland • Sydney
Mexico City • New Delhi • Hong Kong
Danbury, Connecticut

For Tom, who has given me most of the hats I've ever lost.
—C. S.

This book is for my darling daughter Molly.
—R. S.

Reading Consultant

Cecilia Minden-Cupp, PhD
Former Director of the Language and Literacy Program
Harvard Graduate School of Education
Cambridge, Massachusetts

Cover design: The Design Lab
Interior design: Herman Adler

Library of Congress Cataloging-in-Publication Data

Simon, Charnan.
  I've lost my hat / by Charnan Simon ; illustrated by Rick Stromoski.
      p. cm. — (A rookie reader)
  Summary: Rhyming text about a missing hat demonstrates a variety
of prepositions.
  ISBN-10: 0-531-12088-0 (lib. bdg.)   0-531-12490-8 (pbk.)
  ISBN-13: 978-0-531-12088-0 (lib. bdg.)   978-0-531-12490-1 (pbk.)
  [1. Hats—Fiction. 2. English language—Prepositions—Fiction. 3. Stories in rhyme.] I.
Stromoski, Rick, ill. II. Title. III. Title: I have lost my hat. IV. Series.
PZ8.3.S5874Ive 2006
[E] —dc22   2006009118

My hat! My hat! I've lost my hat!

I cannot find my favorite hat!

I think I've looked most everywhere.

Under the bed.

9

Beneath the chair.

Behind the shelf.

On the stairs.

14

I had it at the park with me.

17

It fell off when I climbed a tree.

I stuck it in my pocket, and then . . .

21

I put it on my head again.

I hung it on the hallway rack when . . .

25

I came home to eat my snack.

Where did I put it?
Where could it be?

THERE'S my favorite hat!

Word List (54 words)

(Words in **bold** are prepositions.)

a	climbed	head	my	the
again	could	home	**off**	then
and	did	hung	**on**	there's
at	eat	I	park	think
be	everywhere	**in**	pocket	to
bed	favorite	it	put	tree
behind	fell	I've	rack	**under**
beneath	find	looked	shelf	when
came	had	lost	snack	where
cannot	hallway	me	stairs	**with**
chair	hat	most	stuck	

About the Author

Charnan Simon lives in Madison, Wisconsin, with her husband and two daughters. None of them ever loses a thing.

About the Illustrator

Rick Stromoski wears a lot of hats. His award-winning illustrations appear in children's books, licensing, newspaper syndication, and network television.